Catalog No. 98157
Published by Pomegranate Calendars & Books, Box 6099, Rohnert Park, California 94927
© 1997 Barry Brukoff

Available in Canada from Firefly Books Ltd.,
3680 Victoria Park Avenue, Willowdale, Ontario M2H 3K1
Available in the U.K. and mainland Europe from Pomegranate Europe Ltd.,
Fullbridge House, Fullbridge, Maldon, Essex CM9 7LE, England
Available in Australia from Boobook Publications Pty. Ltd.,
P.O. Box 163 or Freepost 1, Tea Gardens 2324
Available in New Zealand from Randy Horwood Ltd.,
P.O. Box 32-077, Devonport, Auckland
Available in Asia (including the Middle East), Africa, and Latin America from
Pomegranate International Sales, 113 Babcombe Drive, Thornhill, Ontario L3T 1M9, Canada

Pomegranate publishes many other calendars on a variety of subjects, from fine art and
architecture to literature, music, and the environment. Our full-color catalog showing 170 1998
calendars is available for one dollar. We offer our other full-color catalogs (illustrating our
notecards, notecard folios, holiday cards, boxed notes, postcards,
books of postcards, address books, books of days, posters, miniprints,
art magnets, knowledge cards, bookmarks, journals, and books) for nominal fees.
For more information on obtaining catalogs and ordering, please write to
Pomegranate, Box 6099, Rohnert Park, California 94927.

Cover design by Harrah Argentine

PHOTOGRAPHS BY
BARRY BRUKOFF
1998 ENGAGEMENT CALENDAR

Dec/Jan

JANUARY

S	M	T	W	T	F	S
				1	2	3
4	5	6	7	8	9	10
11	12	13	14	15	16	17
18	19	20	21	22	23	24
25	26	27	28	29	30	31

Who can believe that there is no soul behind those luminous eyes!

—Théophile Gautier (1811–1872)

29
New Moon

Monday

30

Tuesday

31

Wednesday

1

1

New Year's Day

Thursday

2

2

Friday

3

3

Saturday

4

4

Sunday

January

S	M	T	W	T	F	S
				1	2	3
4	5	6	7	8	9	10
11	12	13	14	15	16	17
18	19	20	21	22	23	24
25	26	27	28	29	30	31

First Quarter

5

5
Monday

6

6
Tuesday

7

7
Wednesday

8

8
Thursday

9

9
Friday

10

10
Saturday

11

11
Sunday

*I have studied many philosophers
and many cats. The wisdom of cats
is infinitely superior.*

—Hippolyte Taine (1828–1893)

January

S	M	T	W	T	F	S
				1	2	3
4	5	6	7	8	9	10
11	12	13	14	15	16	17
18	19	20	21	22	23	24
25	26	27	28	29	30	31

12

12
Monday

Full Moon

13

13
Tuesday

14

14
Wednesday

15

15
Thursday

Martin Luther King Jr.'s Birthday

16

16
Friday

17

17
Saturday

18

18
Sunday

To Someone very Good and Just,
Who has proved worthy of her
trust,
A Cat will sometimes condescend—
The Dog is Everybody's friend.

—Oliver Herford (1863–1935)

January

S	M	T	W	T	F	S
				1	2	3
4	5	6	7	8	9	10
11	12	13	14	15	16	17
18	19	20	21	22	23	24
25	26	27	28	29	30	31

Martin Luther King Jr.'s Birthday (Observed)

19
Monday

20

20
Tuesday

Last Quarter

21

21
Wednesday

22

22
Thursday

23

23
Friday

24

24
Saturday

25

25
Sunday

*A home without a cat, and a
well-fed, well-patted and properly
revered cat, may be a perfect
home, perhaps, but how can
it prove its title?*

—Mark Twain (1835–1910)

Jan/Feb

FEBRUARY

S	M	T	W	T	F	S
	1	2	3	4	5	6	7
8	9	10	11	12	13	14
15	16	17	18	19	20	21
22	23	24	25	26	27	28

26

26
Monday

27

27
Tuesday

28

New Moon

28
Wednesday

29

29
Thursday

30

30
Friday

31

31
Saturday

32

1
Sunday

Hey diddle, diddle,
The cat and the fiddle,
The cow jumped over the moon;
The little dog laughed
To see such sport,
And the dish ran away with the
*   spoon.*

—Nursery rhyme

February

S	M	T	W	T	F	S
1	2	3	4	5	6	7
8	9	10	11	12	13	14
15	16	17	18	19	20	21
22	23	24	25	26	27	28

2
Monday

34

3

First Quarter

Tuesday

35

4
Wednesday

36

5
Thursday

37

6
Friday

38

7
Saturday

39

The playful kitten with its pretty little tigerish gambole is infinitely more amusing than half the people one is obliged to live with in the world.

—Sydney Morgan (1783–1859)

8
Sunday

February

S	M	T	W	T	F	S
	1	2	3	4	5	6	7
8	9	10	11	12	13	14
15	16	17	18	19	20	21
22	23	24	25	26	27	28

9
Monday

41

10
Tuesday

42

11
Wednesday

Full Moon

43

12
Thursday

Lincoln's Birthday

44

13
Friday

45

14
Saturday

Valentine's Day

46

15
Sunday

When all candles be out,
all cats be gray.
—John Heywood, *Proverbs,* 1546

February

S	M	T	W	T	F	S
	1	2	3	4	5	6	7
8	9	10	11	12	13	14
15	16	17	18	19	20	21
22	23	24	25	26	27	28

Presidents' Day

16
Monday

48

17
Tuesday

49

18
Wednesday

50

19
Thursday

Last Quarter

51

20
Friday

52

21
Saturday

53

I could endure anything before but a cat, and now he's a cat to me.

—William Shakespeare (1564–1616),
All's Well That Ends Well

Washington's Birthday

22
Sunday

Feb/Mar

MARCH

S	M	T	W	T	F	S
1	2	3	4	5	6	7
8	9	10	11	12	13	14
15	16	17	18	19	20	21
22	23	24	25	26	27	28
29	30	31				

23
Monday

24
Tuesday

Ash Wednesday

25
Wednesday

26
Thursday

New Moon

27
Friday

28
Saturday

In a cat's eyes,
all things belong to cats.

—English proverb

1
Sunday

March

S	M	T	W	T	F	S
1	2	3	4	5	6	7
8	9	10	11	12	13	14
15	16	17	18	19	20	21
22	23	24	25	26	27	28
29	30	31				

2 Monday

3 Tuesday

4 Wednesday

First Quarter

5 Thursday

6 Friday

7 Saturday

*When the tea is brought at five
    o'clock,
And all the neat curtains are drawn
    with care,
The little black cat with bright
    green eyes
Is suddenly purring there.*

—Harold Monro (1879–1932),
"Milk for the Cat"

8 Sunday

March

S	M	T	W	T	F	S
1	2	3	4	5	6	7
8	9	10	11	12	13	14
15	16	17	18	19	20	21
22	23	24	25	26	27	28
29	30	31				

9
Monday

10
Tuesday

11
Wednesday

12
Thursday

Full Moon

13
Friday

14
Saturday

We should be careful to get out of an experience only the wisdom that is in it and stop there; lest we be like the cat that sits down on a hot stove-lid. She will never sit down on a hot stove-lid again—and that is well; but also she will never sit down on a cold one.

—Mark Twain (1835–1910)

15
Sunday

March

S	M	T	W	T	F	S
	1	2	3	4	5	6	7
8	9	10	11	12	13	14
15	16	17	18	19	20	21
22	23	24	25	26	27	28
29	30	31				

16
Monday

St. Patrick's Day

17
Tuesday

18
Wednesday

19
Thursday

Vernal Equinox 7:55 P.M. (GMT)

20
Friday

Last Quarter

21
Saturday

Think of her beautiful gliding form,
Her tread that would scarcely crush
*   a worm,*
And her soothing song by the winter
*   fire,*
Soft as the dying throb of a lyre.

*   —William Wordsworth (1770–1850)*

22
Sunday

March

S	M	T	W	T	F	S
1	2	3	4	5	6	7
8	9	10	11	12	13	14
15	16	17	18	19	20	21
22	23	24	25	26	27	28
29	30	31				

23
Monday

24
Tuesday

25
Wednesday

26
Thursday

27
Friday

New Moon

28
Saturday

No matter how much cats fight, there always seem to be plenty of kittens.

—Abraham Lincoln (1809–1865)

29
Sunday

Mar/Apr

APRIL

S	M	T	W	T	F	S
			1	2	3	4
5	6	7	8	9	10	11
12	13	14	15	16	17	18
19	20	21	22	23	24	25
26	27	28	29	30		

30
Monday

31
Tuesday

1
Wednesday

2
Thursday

3
First Quarter

Friday

4
Saturday

What sort of philosophers are we who know absolutely nothing of the origin and destiny of cats?

—Henry David Thoreau (1817–1862)

Palm Sunday

5
Sunday

April

S	M	T	W	T	F	S
			1	2	3	4
5	6	7	8	9	10	11
12	13	14	15	16	17	18
19	20	21	22	23	24	25
26	27	28	29	30		

A cat will never drown if she sees the shore.

—Francis Bacon (1561–1626)

96

6
Monday

97

7
Tuesday

98

8
Wednesday

99

9
Thursday

100

Good Friday
Passover (begins at sundown)

10
Friday

101

Full Moon

11
Saturday

102

Easter Sunday

12
Sunday

April

S	M	T	W	T	F	S
			1	2	3	4
5	6	7	8	9	10	11
12	13	14	15	16	17	18
19	20	21	22	23	24	25
26	27	28	29	30		

13
Monday

Easter Monday (Canada)

14
Tuesday

15
Wednesday

16
Thursday

17
Friday

18
Saturday

19
Sunday

Those who'll play with cats must expect to be scratched.

—Miguel de Cervantes (1547–1616)

Last Quarter

April

S	M	T	W	T	F	S
			1	2	3	4
5	6	7	8	9	10	11
12	13	14	15	16	17	18
19	20	21	22	23	24	25
26	27	28	29	30		

20
Monday

21
Tuesday

Earth Day

22
Wednesday

23
Thursday

24
Friday

25
Saturday

*The cat is mighty dignified
until the dog comes by.*

—Southern folk saying

New Moon

26
Sunday

Apr/May

27
Monday

MAY

S	M	T	W	T	F	S
					1	2
3	4	5	6	7	8	9
10	11	12	13	14	15	16
17	18	19	20	21	22	23
24	25	26	27	28	29	30
31						

28
Tuesday

29
Wednesday

30
Thursday

1
Friday

It's very hard to be polite
  If you're a cat
When other folks are up at table
Eating all that they are able,
  You are down upon the mat
  If you're a cat.

2
Saturday

You're expected just to sit
  If you're a cat
Not to let them know you're there
By scratching on the chair,
Or a light, respected pat
  If you're a cat.

You are not to make a fuss
  If you're a cat
Tho' there's fish upon the plate
You're expected just to wait,
  Wait politely on the mat
  If you're a cat.

—Anonymous

First Quarter

3
Sunday

May

S	M	T	W	T	F	S
					1	2
3	4	5	6	7	8	9
10	11	12	13	14	15	16
17	18	19	20	21	22	23
24	25	26	27	28	29	30
31						

4
Monday

125

5
Tuesday

Cinco de Mayo

126

6
Wednesday

127

7
Thursday

128

8
Friday

129

9
Saturday

130

10
Sunday

Mother's Day

He has gone to fish for his Aunt
    Jobiska's
Runcible Cat with crimson whiskers!

—Edward Lear (1812–1888), *Nonsense
Songs,* "The Pobble who has no Toes"

May

S	M	T	W	T	F	S
					1	2
3	4	5	6	7	8	9
10	11	12	13	14	15	16
17	18	19	20	21	22	23
24	25	26	27	28	29	30
31						

11
Monday

Full Moon

12
Tuesday

13
Wednesday

14
Thursday

15
Friday

16
Saturday

Armed Forces Day

17
Sunday

*My sister crying, our maid howling,
our cat wringing her hands.*

—William Shakespeare (1564–1616),
Two Gentlemen of Verona

May

S	M	T	W	T	F	S
					1	2
3	4	5	6	7	8	9
10	11	12	13	14	15	16
17	18	19	20	21	22	23
24	25	26	27	28	29	30
31						

18
Monday

Victoria Day (Canada)

19
Tuesday

Last Quarter

20
Wednesday

21
Thursday

22
Friday

23
Saturday

24
Sunday

A kitten is so flexible that she is almost double; the hind parts are equivalent to another kitten with which the forepart plays. She does not discover that her tail belongs to her until you tread on it.

—Henry David Thoreau (1817–1862)

May

S	M	T	W	T	F	S
					1	2
3	4	5	6	7	8	9
10	11	12	13	14	15	16
17	18	19	20	21	22	23
24	25	26	27	28	29	30
31						

Memorial Day (Observed)
New Moon

25
Monday

146

26
Tuesday

147

27
Wednesday

148

28
Thursday

149

29
Friday

150

Memorial Day

30
Saturday

151

*She useth therefore to wash her
face with her feet, which she licketh
and moiseneth with her tongue;
and it is observed by some that if
she put her feet beyond the crown
of her head in this kind of washing,
it is a sign of rain.*

—John Swan, *Speculum Mundi*, 1643

31
Sunday

June

S	M	T	W	T	F	S
	1	2	3	4	5	6
7	8	9	10	11	12	13
14	15	16	17	18	19	20
21	22	23	24	25	26	27
28	29	30				

1
Monday

2
First Quarter

Tuesday

3
Wednesday

4
Thursday

5
Friday

6
Saturday

7
Sunday

A little drowsing cat is an image of perfect beatitude.

—Champfleury (Jules Fleury-Husson)
(1821–1889)

June

S	M	T	W	T	F	S
	1	2	3	4	5	6
7	8	9	10	11	12	13
14	15	16	17	18	19	20
21	22	23	24	25	26	27
28	29	30				

8
Monday

9
Tuesday

10
Wednesday

Full Moon

11
Thursday

12
Friday

13
Saturday

14
Sunday

Flag Day

Sing, sing! What shall I sing?
The cat's run away with the
pudding-bag string.

—Anonymous

June

S	M	T	W	T	F	S
	1	2	3	4	5	6
7	8	9	10	11	12	13
14	15	16	17	18	19	20
21	22	23	24	25	26	27
28	29	30				

15
Monday

16
Tuesday

17
Wednesday

Last Quarter

18
Thursday

19
Friday

20
Saturday

Father's Day
Summer Solstice 2:03 P.M. (GMT)

21
Sunday

*Cats love one so much—more than
they will allow. But they have so
much wisdom they keep it to
themselves.*

—Mary E. Wilkins Freeman (1852–1930)

June

S	M	T	W	T	F	S
	1	2	3	4	5	6
7	8	9	10	11	12	13
14	15	16	17	18	19	20
21	22	23	24	25	26	27
28	29	30				

22
Monday

23
Tuesday

24
Wednesday

New Moon

25
Thursday

26
Friday

27
Saturday

28
Sunday

Nothing is so difficult as to paint the cat's face, which as Moncrif justly observes, bears a character of "finesse and hilarity." The lines are so delicate, the eyes so strange, the movements subject to such sudden impulses, that one should be feline oneself to portray such a subject.

—Champfleury (Jules Fleury-Husson)
(1821–1889)

Jun/Jul

JULY

S	M	T	W	T	F	S
			1	2	3	4
5	6	7	8	9	10	11
12	13	14	15	16	17	18
19	20	21	22	23	24	25
26	27	28	29	30	31	

29
Monday

30
Tuesday

Canada Day (Canada)
First Quarter

1
Wednesday

2
Thursday

3
Friday

Stately, kindly, lordly friend,
    Condescend
Here to sit by me, and turn
Glorious eyes that smile and burn,
Golden eyes, love's lustrous meed,
On the golden page I read.

All your wondrous wealth of hair,
    Dark and fair,
Silken-shaggy, soft and bright
As the clouds and beams of night,
Pays my reverent hand's caress
Back with friendlier gentleness.

Dogs may fawn on all and some
    As they come;
You, a friend of loftier mind,
Answer friends alone in kind.
Just your foot upon my hand
Softly bids it understand.

    —A. C. Swinburne (1837–1909),
        "To a Cat"

Independence Day

4
Saturday

5
Sunday

July

S	M	T	W	T	F	S
			1	2	3	4
5	6	7	8	9	10	11
12	13	14	15	16	17	18
19	20	21	22	23	24	25
26	27	28	29	30	31	

6
Monday

7
Tuesday

8
Wednesday

Full Moon

9
Thursday

10
Friday

11
Saturday

In its flawless grace and superior self-sufficiency I have seen a symbol of the perfect beauty and bland impersonality of the universe itself, objectively considered, and in its air of silent mystery there resides for me all the wonder and fascination of the unknown.

—H. P. Lovecraft (1890–1937)

12
Sunday

July

S	M	T	W	T	F	S
			1	2	3	4
5	6	7	8	9	10	11
12	13	14	15	16	17	18
19	20	21	22	23	24	25
26	27	28	29	30	31	

13
Monday

14
Tuesday

15
Wednesday

16
Thursday

Last Quarter

17
Friday

18
Saturday

19
Sunday

Nothing is more playful than a young cat, nor more grave than an old one.
—Thomas Fuller (1608–1661)

July

S	M	T	W	T	F	S
			1	2	3	4
5	6	7	8	9	10	11
12	13	14	15	16	17	18
19	20	21	22	23	24	25
26	27	28	29	30	31	

20
Monday

21
Tuesday

22
Wednesday

New Moon

23
Thursday

24
Friday

25
Saturday

*He loved books, and when he found
one open on the table he would lie
down on it, turn over the edges of
the leaves with his paw, and after
a while, fall asleep, for all the world
as if he had been reading a
fashionable novel.*

—Théophile Gautier (1811–1872)

26
Sunday

Jul/Aug

AUGUST

S	M	T	W	T	F	S
						1
2	3	4	5	6	7	8
9	10	11	12	13	14	15
16	17	18	19	20	21	22
23	24	25	26	27	28	29
30	31					

To please himself only the cat purrs.
—Irish proverb

208

27
Monday

209

28
Tuesday

210

29
Wednesday

211

30
Thursday

212

31
First Quarter
Friday

213

1
Saturday

214

2
Sunday

August

S	M	T	W	T	F	S
						1
2	3	4	5	6	7	8
9	10	11	12	13	14	15
16	17	18	19	20	21	22
23	24	25	26	27	28	29
30	31					

3
Monday

216

4
Tuesday

217

5
Wednesday

218

6
Thursday

219

7
Friday

220

Full Moon

8
Saturday

221

9
Sunday

There are cats and cats.

—Denis Diderot (1713–1784)

August

S	M	T	W	T	F	S
						1
2	3	4	5	6	7	8
9	10	11	12	13	14	15
16	17	18	19	20	21	22
23	24	25	26	27	28	29
30	31					

10
Monday

223

11
Tuesday

224

12
Wednesday

225

13
Thursday

226

Last Quarter

14
Friday

227

15
Saturday

228

16
Sunday

One of the most striking differences between a cat and a lie is that a cat has only nine lives.
—Mark Twain (1835–1910)

August

S	M	T	W	T	F	S
						1
2	3	4	5	6	7	8
9	10	11	12	13	14	15
16	17	18	19	20	21	22
23	24	25	26	27	28	29
30	31					

17
Monday

230

18
Tuesday

231

19
Wednesday

232

20
Thursday

233

21
Friday

234

New Moon

22
Saturday

235

When I play with my cat, who knows whether she is not amusing herself with me more than I with her?

—Michel de Montaigne (1533–1592)

23
Sunday

August

S	M	T	W	T	F	S
						1
2	3	4	5	6	7	8
9	10	11	12	13	14	15
16	17	18	19	20	21	22
23	24	25	26	27	28	29
30	31					

24
Monday

25
Tuesday

26
Wednesday

27
Thursday

28
Friday

29
Saturday

First Quarter

30
Sunday

The cat, with eyes of burning coal,
Now couches 'fore the mouse's hole.

—William Shakespeare (1564–1616),
Pericles, Prince of Tyre

Aug/Sep

SEPTEMBER

S	M	T	W	T	F	S
		1	2	3	4	5
6	7	8	9	10	11	12
13	14	15	16	17	18	19
20	21	22	23	24	25	26
27	28	29	30			

31
Monday

1
Tuesday

2
Wednesday

3
Thursday

4
Friday

5
Saturday

I love little pussy
Her coat is so warm;
And if I don't hurt her
She'll do me no harm.

—Nursery rhyme

Full Moon

6
Sunday

September

S	M	T	W	T	F	S
		1	2	3	4	5
6	7	8	9	10	11	12
13	14	15	16	17	18	19
20	21	22	23	24	25	26
27	28	29	30			

Labor Day (U.S. and Canada)

7
Monday

8
Tuesday

9
Wednesday

10
Thursday

11
Friday

12
Saturday

You could never accuse him of idleness, and yet he knew the secret of repose.

—Charles Dudley Warner (1829–1900)

Last Quarter

13
Sunday

September

S	M	T	W	T	F	S
		1	2	3	4	5
6	7	8	9	10	11	12
13	14	15	16	17	18	19
20	21	22	23	24	25	26
27	28	29	30			

14
Monday

15
Tuesday

16
Wednesday

17
Thursday

18
Friday

19
Saturday

The way to keep a cat is to try to chase it away.
—E. W. Howe (1853–1937)

Rosh Hashanah (begins at sundown)
New Moon

20
Sunday

September

S	M	T	W	T	F	S
		1	2	3	4	5
6	7	8	9	10	11	12
13	14	15	16	17	18	19
20	21	22	23	24	25	26
27	28	29	30			

21
Monday

265

22
Tuesday

266

23
Wednesday

Autumnal Equinox 5:37 A.M. (GMT)

267

24
Thursday

268

25
Friday

269

26
Saturday

270

27
Sunday

*The ideal of calm
exists in a sitting cat.*

—Jules Renard (1864–1910)

Sep/Oct

28
Monday

First Quarter

29
Tuesday

Yom Kippur (begins at sundown)

OCTOBER

S	M	T	W	T	F	S
				1	2	3
4	5	6	7	8	9	10
11	12	13	14	15	16	17
18	19	20	21	22	23	24
25	26	27	28	29	30	31

30
Wednesday

1
Thursday

2
Friday

3
Saturday

If a dog jumps into your lap, it is because he is fond of you; but if a cat does the same thing, it is because your lap is warmer.

—Alfred North Whitehead (1861–1947)

4
Sunday

October

S	M	T	W	T	F	S
				1	2	3
4	5	6	7	8	9	10
11	12	13	14	15	16	17
18	19	20	21	22	23	24
25	26	27	28	29	30	31

Full Moon

5
Monday

6
Tuesday

7
Wednesday

8
Thursday

9
Friday

10
Saturday

11
Sunday

The cat is the only animal that accepts the comforts but rejects the bondage of domesticity.

—Georges Louis Leclerc de Buffon
(1707–1788)

October

S	M	T	W	T	F	S
				1	2	3
4	5	6	7	8	9	10
11	12	13	14	15	16	17
18	19	20	21	22	23	24
25	26	27	28	29	30	31

Columbus Day
Thanksgiving Day (Canada)
Last Quarter

12
Monday

13
Tuesday

14
Wednesday

15
Thursday

16
Friday

17
Saturday

18
Sunday

Always well-behaved am I,
Never scratch and never cry;
Only touch the diner's hand,
So that he can understand
That I want a modest share
Of the good things that are there.
If he pay but scanty heed
To my little stomach's need,
I beg him with a mew polite
To give me just a single bite.
Greedy though that diner be,
He will share his meal with me.

—Antoinette Deshoulières (1638–1694)

October

S	M	T	W	T	F	S
				1	2	3
4	5	6	7	8	9	10
11	12	13	14	15	16	17
18	19	20	21	22	23	24
25	26	27	28	29	30	31

19
Monday

New Moon

20
Tuesday

21
Wednesday

22
Thursday

23
Friday

United Nations Day

24
Saturday

The cat, an aristocrat, merits our esteem, while the dog is only a scurvy type who got his position by low flatteries.

—Alexandre Dumas (1812–1870)

25
Sunday

Oct/Nov

26

Monday

27

Tuesday

NOVEMBER

S	M	T	W	T	F	S
	1	2	3	4	5	6	7
8	9	10	11	12	13	14
15	16	17	18	19	20	21
22	23	24	25	26	27	28
29	30					

28

Wednesday

First Quarter

29

Thursday

30

Friday

31

Saturday

Halloween

1

Sunday

*The cat loves fish,
but hates wet feet.*

—Medieval proverb

November

S	M	T	W	T	F	S
	1	2	3	4	5	6	7
1	2	3	4	5	6	7
8	9	10	11	12	13	14
15	16	17	18	19	20	21
22	23	24	25	26	27	28
29	30

2
Monday

Election Day

3
Tuesday

Full Moon

4
Wednesday

5
Thursday

6
Friday

7
Saturday

"Please would you tell me," said Alice a little timidly, . . . "why your cat grins like that?" "It's a Cheshire cat," said the Duchess, "and that's why."

—Lewis Carroll (1832–1898),
Alice's Adventures in Wonderland

8
Sunday

November

S	M	T	W	T	F	S
1	2	3	4	5	6	7
8	9	10	11	12	13	14
15	16	17	18	19	20	21
22	23	24	25	26	27	28
29	30					

9
Monday

10
Tuesday

Veterans Day
Remembrance Day (Canada)
Last Quarter

11
Wednesday

12
Thursday

13
Friday

14
Saturday

15
Sunday

It is difficult to obtain the friendship of a cat. It is a philosophic animal, strange, holding to its habits, friend of order and cleanliness and one that does not place its affections thoughtlessly. It wishes only to be your friend (if you are worthy) and not your slave. It retains its free will and will do nothing for that it considers unreasonable.

—Théophile Gautier (1811–1872)

November

S	M	T	W	T	F	S
1	2	3	4	5	6	7
8	9	10	11	12	13	14
15	16	17	18	19	20	21
22	23	24	25	26	27	28
29	30					

16
Monday

321

17
Tuesday

322

18
Wednesday

323

19
Thursday

New Moon

324

20
Friday

325

21
Saturday

326

22
Sunday

*Cats make exquisite photographs.
They don't keep bouncing at you to
be kissed just as you get the lens
adjusted.*

—Gladys Taber, *Ladies' Home Journal*,
October 1941

November

S	M	T	W	T	F	S
	1	2	3	4	5	6	7
8	9	10	11	12	13	14
15	16	17	18	19	20	21
22	23	24	25	26	27	28
29	30					

23
Monday

24
Tuesday

25
Wednesday

Thanksgiving Day

26
Thursday

First Quarter

27
Friday

28
Saturday

29
Sunday

*Lat take a cat and fostre hym wel
    with milk
And tendre flessch and make his
    couche of silk,
And lat hym seen a mouse go by
    the wal,
Anon he weyvith milk and flessch
    and al,
And every deyntee that is in that
    hous,
Suich appetit he hath to ete a
    mous.*

—Geoffrey Chaucer (c. 1342–1400),
    from *The Manciple's Tale*

Nov/Dec

DECEMBER

S	M	T	W	T	F	S
		1	2	3	4	5
6	7	8	9	10	11	12
13	14	15	16	17	18	19
20	21	22	23	24	25	26
27	28	29	30	31		

30
Monday

335

1
Tuesday

336

2
Wednesday

337

3
Thursday

Full Moon

338

4
Friday

339

5
Saturday

340

6
Sunday

The smallest feline is a masterpiece.
—Leonardo da Vinci (1452–1519)

December

S	M	T	W	T	F	S
		1	2	3	4	5
6	7	8	9	10	11	12
13	14	15	16	17	18	19
20	21	22	23	24	25	26
27	28	29	30	31		

7
Monday

8
Tuesday

9
Wednesday

Last Quarter

10
Thursday

11
Friday

12
Saturday

Cats know how to obtain food without labor, shelter without confinement and love without penalties.

—Walter Lionel George (1882–1926)

Hanukkah (begins at sundown)

13
Sunday

December

S	M	T	W	T	F	S
		1	2	3	4	5
6	7	8	9	10	11	12
13	14	15	16	17	18	19
20	21	22	23	24	25	26
27	28	29	30	31		

14
Monday

15
Tuesday

16
Wednesday

17
Thursday

New Moon

18
Friday

19
Saturday

If man could be crossed with a cat,
it would improve man but
deteriorate the cat.

—Mark Twain (1835–1910)

20
Sunday

December

S	M	T	W	T	F	S
		1	2	3	4	5
6	7	8	9	10	11	12
13	14	15	16	17	18	19
20	21	22	23	24	25	26
27	28	29	30	31		

21
Monday

22
Tuesday

Winter Solstice 1:56 A.M. (GMT)

23
Wednesday

24
Thursday

25
Friday

Christmas Day

26
Saturday

Boxing Day (Canada)
First Quarter

27
Sunday

*Cats are a mysterious kind of folk.
There is more passing in their
minds than we are aware of.*

—Sir Walter Scott (1771–1832)

Dec/Jan

JANUARY

S	M	T	W	T	F	S
					1	2
3	4	5	6	7	8	9
10	11	12	13	14	15	16
17	18	19	20	21	22	23
24	25	26	27	28	29	30
31						

28
Monday

29
Tuesday

30
Wednesday

31
Thursday

1

1
New Year's Day, 1999

Friday

2

2
Full Moon

Saturday

3

3
Sunday

Ignorant people think it's the noise which fighting cats make that is so aggravating, but it ain't so; it's the disgusting grammar they use.

—Mark Twain (1835–1910)

1998 year at a glance

JANUARY

S	M	T	W	T	F	S
				1	2	3
4	5	6	7	8	9	10
11	12	13	14	15	16	17
18	19	20	21	22	23	24
25	26	27	28	29	30	31

MAY

S	M	T	W	T	F	S
					1	2
3	4	5	6	7	8	9
10	11	12	13	14	15	16
17	18	19	20	21	22	23
24	25	26	27	28	29	30
31						

SEPTEMBER

S	M	T	W	T	F	S
		1	2	3	4	5
6	7	8	9	10	11	12
13	14	15	16	17	18	19
20	21	22	23	24	25	26
27	28	29	30			

FEBRUARY

S	M	T	W	T	F	S
1	2	3	4	5	6	7
8	9	10	11	12	13	14
15	16	17	18	19	20	21
22	23	24	25	26	27	28

JUNE

S	M	T	W	T	F	S
	1	2	3	4	5	6
7	8	9	10	11	12	13
14	15	16	17	18	19	20
21	22	23	24	25	26	27
28	29	30				

OCTOBER

S	M	T	W	T	F	S
				1	2	3
4	5	6	7	8	9	10
11	12	13	14	15	16	17
18	19	20	21	22	23	24
25	26	27	28	29	30	31

MARCH

S	M	T	W	T	F	S
1	2	3	4	5	6	7
8	9	10	11	12	13	14
15	16	17	18	19	20	21
22	23	24	25	26	27	28
29	30	31				

JULY

S	M	T	W	T	F	S
			1	2	3	4
5	6	7	8	9	10	11
12	13	14	15	16	17	18
19	20	21	22	23	24	25
26	27	28	29	30	31	

NOVEMBER

S	M	T	W	T	F	S
1	2	3	4	5	6	7
8	9	10	11	12	13	14
15	16	17	18	19	20	21
22	23	24	25	26	27	28
29	30					

APRIL

S	M	T	W	T	F	S
			1	2	3	4
5	6	7	8	9	10	11
12	13	14	15	16	17	18
19	20	21	22	23	24	25
26	27	28	29	30		

AUGUST

S	M	T	W	T	F	S
						1
2	3	4	5	6	7	8
9	10	11	12	13	14	15
16	17	18	19	20	21	22
23	24	25	26	27	28	29
30	31					

DECEMBER

S	M	T	W	T	F	S
		1	2	3	4	5
6	7	8	9	10	11	12
13	14	15	16	17	18	19
20	21	22	23	24	25	26
27	28	29	30	31		

JANUARY

S	M	T	W	T	F	S
					1	2
3	4	5	6	7	8	9
10	11	12	13	14	15	16
17	18	19	20	21	22	23
24	25	26	27	28	29	30
31						

MAY

S	M	T	W	T	F	S
						1
2	3	4	5	6	7	8
9	10	11	12	13	14	15
16	17	18	19	20	21	22
23	24	25	26	27	28	29
30	31					

SEPTEMBER

S	M	T	W	T	F	S
			1	2	3	4
5	6	7	8	9	10	11
12	13	14	15	16	17	18
19	20	21	22	23	24	25
26	27	28	29	30		

FEBRUARY

S	M	T	W	T	F	S
	1	2	3	4	5	6
7	8	9	10	11	12	13
14	15	16	17	18	19	20
21	22	23	24	25	26	27
28						

JUNE

S	M	T	W	T	F	S
		1	2	3	4	5
6	7	8	9	10	11	12
13	14	15	16	17	18	19
20	21	22	23	24	25	26
27	28	29	30			

OCTOBER

S	M	T	W	T	F	S
					1	2
3	4	5	6	7	8	9
10	11	12	13	14	15	16
17	18	19	20	21	22	23
24	25	26	27	28	29	30
31						

MARCH

S	M	T	W	T	F	S
	1	2	3	4	5	6
7	8	9	10	11	12	13
14	15	16	17	18	19	20
21	22	23	24	25	26	27
28	29	30	31			

JULY

S	M	T	W	T	F	S
				1	2	3
4	5	6	7	8	9	10
11	12	13	14	15	16	17
18	19	20	21	22	23	24
25	26	27	28	29	30	31

NOVEMBER

S	M	T	W	T	F	S
	1	2	3	4	5	6
7	8	9	10	11	12	13
14	15	16	17	18	19	20
21	22	23	24	25	26	27
28	29	30				

APRIL

S	M	T	W	T	F	S
				1	2	3
4	5	6	7	8	9	10
11	12	13	14	15	16	17
18	19	20	21	22	23	24
25	26	27	28	29	30	

AUGUST

S	M	T	W	T	F	S
1	2	3	4	5	6	7
8	9	10	11	12	13	14
15	16	17	18	19	20	21
22	23	24	25	26	27	28
29	30	31				

DECEMBER

S	M	T	W	T	F	S
			1	2	3	4
5	6	7	8	9	10	11
12	13	14	15	16	17	18
19	20	21	22	23	24	25
26	27	28	29	30	31	

Notes

Notes

Notes